Praise for Sonja Radvila's *Young Yogi and the Mind M*

This delightful children's story is for everyone: young, m⸺ ⸺y. Join Young Yogi as innocence fades away and he makes the journey ⸺iscovery. Thoughts shape reality; Young Yogi learns how to play with the mind, awake and in dream, plumb the depths of the ocean and rise above it all. The craft of illustrated storytelling comes alive here, with lessons on the power of Yoga in abundance on every page!

Christopher Key Chapple, Doshi Professor of Indic and Comparative Theology
Director, Master of Arts in Yoga Studies, Loyola Marymount University
Author of *Yoga and the Luminous: Patañjali's Spiritual Path to Freedom*

In his *Yoga Sūtras*, Patañjali presents a philosophy that we are not this restless and ever dissatisfied mind, but pure consciousness at our deepest core. But as every parent knows, young children are especially challenged to separate themselves from the volatility and pressures of their emotions and desires.

Loosely and creatively following the sequence of the first chapter of the Sūtras, *Young Yogi and the Mind Monsters* is a richly evocative and captivating tale that will be welcomed by yogi parents seeking tools to instill Patañjali's seemingly daunting yoga philosophy into their children. Through a series of very lively and fun-filled adventures suitable for young children, the story presents the conceptual framework of the teachings – that our ultimate natures are distinct from the impulses of this monster mind, which so frequently acts against our best interests – along with practical techniques as to how to control it. Another welcome example of yoga philosophy's inherent ability to benevolently affect all areas of our modern world, including, in this Tale, our most precious one, the minds of our children.

Edwin Bryant, Professor of Hinduism, Rutgers University
Author of *The Yoga Sūtras of Patañjali: A New Edition, Translation, and Commentary*

Sonja's new book brings the Yoga Sūtras to life in a brilliant re-imagining that captures their meaning in surprising ways at each turn. It is both a wonderful introduction to this fundamental yoga text and also a means to rediscover it anew, bringing us on a journey through these ancient sayings. Every page of the story is a joy, accompanied by beautiful, colorful, vibrant illustrations. Having spent many years reading, translating, and discussing the sūtras, I know it is not easy to convey their essence in an understandable way. Though written as a book for children, this book is a treasure for adults, too. I am already hoping there will be a sequel to take us through the rest of the Yoga Sūtras!

Zoë Slatoff, Author of *Yogāvatāraṇam: The Translation of Yoga*
PhD candidate

Sonja Radvila's retelling of the *Yoga Sūtras* captivates the hearts and minds of children and adult seekers alike. This joyful one-of-a-kind story takes the reader to the essence of the yogic wisdom in a lucid as well as relatable way. Along with the exquisite illustrations, Young Yogi's exploration into our ability to break free from suffering and find peace in life is a true must read.

Sharmila Desai, Founder of Ashtanga Yoga Morjim, Co-Author of *Yoga Sadhana for Mothers: Shared Experiences of Ashtanga Yoga, Pregnancy, Birth & Motherhood*

Sonja and Kaori have done something amazing. They have made the *Yoga Sūtras* accessible for kids and badly educated adults (me). With the awareness of mental health issues in kids, this book gives keys to unlock doors to happiness, understanding the mind and peace, which are the same thing. Patañjali's *Yoga Sūtras* are notoriously difficult to understand with the many commentaries available. This new understanding gives light where there is darkness.

Hamish Hendry, Author of *Yoga Dharma*, Founder of Ashtanga Yoga London

Young Yogi and the Mind Monsters

written by Sonja Radvila
illustrated by Kaori Hamura Long

For Happy

Foreword

The revival of yoga is a blessing, not simply for its clear benefits to health but also for its enriching philosophy and guidance for daily life.

In this delightful book, the timeless wisdom of Patañjali's *Yoga Sūtras* is presented in the form of a children's story.

The original text is from ancient India and shares a practical exposition of the philosophy and practice of yoga. However, its sutra form usually requires some elaboration and explanation in order to glean full meaning.

In Sonja Radvila's retelling of Samādhi Pada, the first book of Patañjali's *Yoga Sūtras*, we are offered a spiritual gem, an insightful and accessible companion for parents, children, and seekers of self-knowledge.

Join Young Yogi in his battles with the "Mind Monsters."

Be entertained by his adventures and discoveries as he is introduced to the teachings and practices of yoga. Travel inward together toward self-mastery and freedom whilst unraveling the mysteries of the mind, the nature of the self, and the wonder of the world we reside in.

This work is the fruit of seeds planted during intensive study of Patañjali's *Yoga Sūtras* in Byron Bay, Australia.

I trust you will enjoy this contemporary interpretation of eternal wisdom for the young and young at heart. May it nourish and inspire questioning minds and guide all toward spiritual prosperity and peace.

Dena Kingsberg
Practitioner and teacher in the lineage of Patañjali and K. P. Jois

Author's Note

Young Yogi and the Mind Monsters is my attempt to describe Patañjali's Samādhi Pada, the first chapter in his *Yoga Sūtras*, as a story that even a child could understand. It has been my great challenge to create a tale that not only depicts the essence of each sutra but also follows the order in which they were originally written. You'll find every sutra annotated throughout the book, so that you can easily refer to a more traditional interpretation in the provided appendix, and compare it with Young Yogi's version.

It is my hope that this book offers a fun and light look at the essence of Patañjali, whose multi-layered philosophy is rich, complex, and daunting. I take responsibility for any shortcomings and outright mistakes, for they are mine alone. Please accept this offering as it is intended, from the heart.

Prologue: An Ordinary Boy

There once was a boy like any other. He lived near the sandy shores of Coconut Grove, a bustling town in an unusual land far away. You may have heard of it? It's famous for its high-speed rickshaws and roadside world cuisine, surfers and saints, holy cows and magic meadows, flying monkeys and talking chickens, amongst other strange phenomena. The boy went about his life quite happily there, without a care in the world, really.

Until one day, without even realizing what was happening, he began to believe the thoughts in his mind.

Since he didn't notice at first, he never thought to ask who or what may be causing him to doubt and fear and worry. And so, his life carried on, only it was no longer carefree. He was no longer happy as he used to be. He began to notice. Little did the boy, our Young Yogi, know that his torment would lead him on a journey, and that the journey would lead him to the answers, and the answers would lead him to. . . well, this is just the prologue after all!

The Nightmare

Now one moonlit night, Young Yogi was sleeping peacefully in his room when a stinking cloud seeped under the door and began to take shape over the bed. Paco, his trusty stuffed chicken, ruffled his feathers next to him and in his sleep, stuffed his beak far into the pillow to avoid the stench. The smell reeked of rotten eggs, rubbish, and corn chips all at the same time, and it woke Young Yogi up.

"Paco! Was that you? What's that awful smell?" asked Young Yogi.

"I didn't do it!" argued the grumpy chicken. "You always think—" He was interrupted.

"BAM! BAM! BAM!" The closet door nearly burst open from the sound. It was hard to see for sure since the stinking cloud had consumed the room.

"Uh, Paco," stammered Young Yogi, "there's, uh, something in the closet, um, I think."

"Something or someone!" yelled the chicken.

They were petrified and woozy. Young Yogi gulped as he got off the bed and began slowly walking toward the closet. He felt like he just got off the Mr. Spinny

ride at the amusement park and couldn't keep his balance. Paco hopped on his head, which didn't help either. Just as Young Yogi began reaching for the doorknob, the door was thrust open by two horrifying monsters!

"No!" screamed Young Yogi. He and Paco turned to run from the giant monsters and their snarling teeth, cloudy stench, and dripping goop. Young Yogi managed one more word:

"Help!"

Suddenly, his eyes opened. He heard the click of a switch and with the light saw his parents enter the room.

"Wake up, Yogi!" said Mama Yogini, rushing toward his bed.

"You've had a nightmare," said his father. Young Yogi could hardly catch his breath; he felt confused and upset. How could something *that* real be a dream? Paco lay limply beside him, like any other stuffed animal.

"I can't take it anymore!" said Young Yogi. "I'm never going to sleep again." Nightmares were as common as chores in the Yogi household lately; they were happening all the time. Young Yogi put Paco in his lap as his mom held him in her arms. He felt embarrassed as tears came. Papa Yogi sat at the end of the bed.

[1.1] "It's time," he said, looking over at Mama Yogini.

"Time for what?" asked Young Yogi.

"Well," continued Papa, "these monsters scaring you night after night are a sure sign you're ready to learn the ways of yoga."

"Do you want to make the monsters go away?" asked Mama, wiping his tears.

"Yes," said Young Yogi, "I don't want these monsters and their nightmares around ever again."

[1.2] "This might sound crazy, Yogi," said Papa, "but did you know the monsters are just made up from your mind?"

"And yoga is like magic," added Mama. "It can make anything the mind creates go away—poof! Just like that." She snapped her fingers. Papa nodded. Young Yogi shook his head in doubt. How could the monsters be made-up? That was impossible.

"No, I can't believe it," he said. "They seemed so real. They were going to get me!"

"That's why the mind is powerful," said Mama, "because these things seem so very real."

"Mind is a monster!" added Papa. "But it's a wild beast you can learn to tame."

"I just don't see how, Papa," said Yogi, feeling defeated, tired, and still shaky from the nightmare.

[1.3] "Okay," said Mama, "close your eyes and just *pretend* for a moment that there are no monsters."

"I'll try," said Yogi. He leaned back into his pillow.

"What does it feel like?" she asked. Young Yogi had a hard time shaking the thought of the monsters. He could feel his heart beating in his feet. It didn't feel different at all.

"Take some deep breaths, Yogi. Nice and easy," said Papa. Young Yogi began to calm down. His mind was flitting this way and that at first, but then an image began to take hold. He found himself atop a great mountain, and with a bird's-eye view of the vast land below, he took off, soaring freely over the great peaks and valleys.

"I'm like a bird," he said, "free and calm. And, I'm not afraid of anything!"

"That's right," said Papa, happy for his son.

Young Yogi flew over an enormous volcano and suddenly lost his concentration when he saw a figure down below. It was the local bully, Bharat! How could that be? Before he realized he was over the mouth of the volcano, a slimy monster suddenly snatched Young Yogi from the sky with its large and sloppy tentacles! The beast was just about to gobble him up, and he could hear Bharat laughing at him, when Yogi gasped and opened his eyes.

[1.4] "See that, son!" said Papa. "Don't you see? Without the monsters, there is no problem. But when you believe that they are real, then they have power. And, you are upset."

"Yeah, I'm scared again," said Young Yogi. "It's not just the monster, Bharat was there too."

"That's because Mind Monsters appear not just in nightmares, but in waking life too," said Papa Yogi. "Especially in the people or places we fear most."

"They can be found everywhere," added Mama Yogini.

Young Yogi felt puzzled and tired. Could he really learn to tame what happened in his mind, which seemed so real? Mama Yogini stroked his head as he settled back into the pillow. She tucked the blankets around him. He would think more about it tomorrow, feeling his eyelids become heavy.

"I kind of get what you're saying," he whispered, turning over on his side.

"I think you do," said Mama Yogi, "and I think that's enough for tonight." Young Yogi was lightly snoring. Mama and Papa got up quietly and turned off the light, leaving the door slightly ajar.

"Night, night, my love," she said.

Young Yogi's beginning to explore and question his mind, thought Papa, with a sense of pride. "He is a yogi now," he said, looking back at the sleeping boy.

Monkey Business

Early the next morning Young Yogi heard a tap-tap at his window. "Rise and shine, Young Yogi! Yesh, rise and shine!" said Pascal. The local mischief-maker happened to be one of the most clever and agile monkeys in Coconut Grove. He had a special gift for flying into people's kitchens and eating all their food, which he must have already done since Young Yogi noticed the banana he was carrying.

"Let's go for a ride! Yesh, a ride!" Pascal's favorite word was *yes*, and yesh, he said it all the time, just like that.

Young Yogi wiped his eyes. "No way, Pascal. I hardly got any sleep last night." Noticing the sun barely peaking over the horizon, he pulled the blankets over his head.

"Mind Monsters! No sleep! Yesh! No sleep for you!" laughed the monkey, twirling from his tail. "They have some mind tricks up their furry sleeves, yesh! Oh, yesh they do!"

[1.5] "Mind tricks?" asked Young Yogi, looking out from the covers, curiously. "What are you talking about?"

The monkey took a bite from the banana. "Everyone knows there are many Mind Monsters." He chewed more slowly to hold the suspense. "Mmm, yesh! This is a mighty good banana, yesh . . . but not everyone knows that there are only five mind tricks. Yesh!"

"Five?" asked Young Yogi in disbelief. "How is that possible? No way, I don't believe you."

"Yesh! Believe me, Yogi. Believe me, why would Pascal lie?" He swung from his lanky tail and flipped into the room landing on Young Yogi's bed. Then he did something quite unexpected and pinched Yogi's cheek.

"Ow!" shrieked Young Yogi. "What did you do that for?"

Pascal chuckled. "Five mind tricks, Yogi. And they can either hurt or not. Yesh! I'm sorry to hurt your cheek." Then the monkey gave him a slobbery kiss on the other cheek.

"Ew!" said Young Yogi, wiping the wet monkey kiss off his face. He was getting annoyed. "So let me get this straight, Pascal. There are Mind Monsters, and there are mind tricks."

"Yesh, Yogi. Yesh!" The monkey jumped up and down on the bed.

"And you're telling me that the Mind Monsters have only *five* mind tricks?"

"Yesh! Yesh!" Pascal was beside himself with excitement and circled at high

speed dangling from the ceiling fan. He grabbed Young Yogi from the bed. "Hold on, Young Yogi!" They spun around the room together, flying out of the window into the trees. Young Yogi managed to grab Paco at the last second.

Pascal reached with his long arms through the trees. "Five isn't so many," said Yogi holding tightly to the monkey.

[1.6] "I wonder what they are?" asked Paco nervously, trying not to look down. He really didn't like heights.

"Yesh! Pascal knows. Yesh, I do!" cried the monkey, climbing the tallest coconut tree in the neighborhood. "Mind Monsters' weapon is thoughts, Yogi! Yesh, it's thoughts they use. Clever, yesh!"

"Umm, okay," replied Yogi, as they found a seat atop a high palm tree. "So they use my head?" He was getting curious again.

"Yesh, and everyone else's too," Pascal chuckled. "If you let them, that is." They overlooked the land from the treetop. He grabbed a coconut and gnawed it open. "Now with some mind tricks, the thoughts are true. Yesh, true!" He gulped the coconut water like a parched camel in the desert.

"And some are false. Yesh, false!" He handed Young Yogi and Paco some coconut meat. "And some are pretend. Yesh. They are just pretend."

Young Yogi counted on his fingers. "But that's only three."

"Oooh, smart Yogi. Yesh! Very smart." laughed Pascal, and suddenly he fell asleep on the branch, snoring loudly as his lips flapped together. Then without warning, he fell backward off the branch! Young Yogi and Paco gasped as they watched the monkey drop toward the ground.

It was only a prank. Pascal hung from his tail and yelled from below, "And, sleep!

Sleep can trick you too. Yesh, like the monsters coming by to visit you last night." They looked down bewildered.

Instantly, Pascal swung back up beside them, wearing thin wire-rimmed glasses and a pointy, gray beard. He looked like an old nutty professor. Yogi and Paco sat down on a rather comfortable sofa that appeared on the branch. He pulled out a notebook, and while stroking his beard, in a deep voice said, "Tell me old chap, of your Mind Monster memories." Feeling quite relaxed, Young Yogi began to recall the memories from his nightmares and was about to speak.

Pascal interrupted, "Yesh, memory, dear boy. I daresay memory is also a trick of the mind. Indeed!" He laughed uncontrollably at his antics and snatched the two. Before they knew it, they were swinging in the trees again. Young Yogi and Pascal could hardly keep up with this crazy monkey.

"Okay, Pascal," said Young Yogi losing his breath, "so the Mind Monsters use sleep and memory, too. I think I get that. But what I don't get is how you can tell a true thought from a mind trick."

"Yeah," gulped Paco, clinging to Yogi's shirt, "good question!" He felt squeamish flying so high in the treetops.

[1.7] "Pascal knows! Yesh, I do. True ones you can see with your very own eyes. Yesh, with your own eyes!" And with his own eyes, Pascal spotted what appeared to be a basket of mangoes in a heap of rubbish down below. "Yesh! Mango! Mango!" Young Yogi and Paco held the monkey tightly as he darted for the garbage on the ground. The crazed monkey tossed his glasses aside and gleefully rummaged through the basket, grabbing the largest mango he could find. He licked his lips.

"True ones I see myself, like this mango here. Yesh, I see you mango," he said, salivating, then took a bite.

"Bleh!" His spit it out in disgust and furiously stomped on the plastic bits on the ground, "Fake mango! Yesh! It's a fake mango." Young Yogi and Paco watched with their mouths agape. But Pascal didn't stay angry for long.

"Yesh! True ones are tricky too!" Pascal said laughing again, "Yesh, they can fool you just the same. But Pascal is no fool for long. Oh no. Yesh!" He bounced himself into the middle of the road and sat there.

"Uh, Pascal, uh, I don't think that's really a good idea," said Young Yogi, concerned. He looked at Paco, who gulped. It was no use, the monkey had a point to make. He lay on his back and began juggling a giant globe with his feet.

"Maybe you didn't know, Yogi. But in the olden days, they thought the Earth was a flat place. Yesh, flat! Just like this." Just then a car came zooming down the road, and instead of running to the side, Pascal flattened himself into a pancake as the car passed over him. He sprung up delighted with himself. Young Yogi froze at the close call.

"Kids, don't try this at home!" Yelled Paco, flapping his wings.

"Flat! No splat! See? Don't worry Yogi. C'mon! Yesh, c'mon!" said Pascal ready for the next adventure. Young Yogi had had enough of this daredevil monkey for one day.

"I think I better get home now, Pascal. My mom will be worried."

"Okay, Yogi. Yesh, okay," said the disappointed monkey. They were off again into the tree, and as they neared Young Yogi's house, the sky began to darken and sounds of thunder emerged in the distance.

"Young Yogi!" called Mama Yogini, waving toward the treetops. "You're just in time to help me get this laundry inside." Pascal scooted down the long tree trunk, and Young Yogi and Paco hopped off his back. Pascal bowed to Mama Yogini, and she patted him on the head.

"It looks like it's going to rain," said Young Yogi smelling the damp air. It felt good to have his feet on the ground.

"Yesh! Smart guess, Yogi. Yesh, that's a smart guess," chuckled Pascal swinging from the laundry line.

"Pascal! Don't you dare break my clothesline!" scolded Mama Yogini with a smile. No one was ever really mad at the cheeky monkey. They managed to get inside just as the rain poured and the thunder roared. Pascal swung into the trees waving good-bye.

Snakes and Ladders

The rain continued to fall, and Young Yogi found Papa Yogi in the study reading as he sat in lotus on the floor. "Papa, I've just learned that there are only five mind tricks." Papa looked up with interest.

"That's right, son."

"And I learned that even the mind tricks that seem true can be tricks too!"

"That's correct, Young Yogi," said Papa nodding with approval. "I'm happy to see you showing an interest." He set his book aside, got up, and walked toward his towering bookshelf.

"There's something else," he continued gesturing to his shelves of books. "True thoughts can come from a source you can count on—like a trusted book or a person who really knows something." Papa climbed high up his ladder, reaching for an old dusty volume.

"Like Mr. Siva or Professor Parvati at school?" asked Young Yogi, thinking of the smartest people he knew. He looked up at his father.

"Yes," answered Papa, perusing more titles.

[1.8] "Then Papa, what about the false ones? What are they?"

"Those are the ones in which something false seems to be true. It's a real trick!" Papa exclaimed, descending the ladder easily with three heavy, oversized books.

"It's just like when people think I'm just a stuffed chicken full of cotton and beans," whispered Paco in Yogi's ear. He understood not everything is as it seems.

"Young Yogi," called Mama, "the rain stopped. Can you come help me in the shed?"

"You better go help your mother," said Papa, sitting back down with his books. "We can talk more mind tricks later."

 "Yogi, I need you to help me move this box outside," said Mama. They carried the heavy box to the shed and opened the door. It was dark and musty inside. Mama Yogini walked with a start.

"Ooh!" she shrieked. "There's a sn-snake!"

"Where, Mama? Where?" Young Yogi asked. His heart thumped loudly in his chest. He dropped the box and turned on the light.

"Mama! It's just a rope!" They looked on the floor, and sure enough it was a coiled-up old rope laying there. Mama looked at Yogi and started to laugh.

"See, Young Yogi! Another mind trick!"

"They're everywhere, Mama!" They were still laughing as they walked back to the house. Young Yogi twirled the rope like a lasso. "I think I'm starting to understand these mind tricks a little better," he said winking, jumping through the lasso loops. The sun began to shine again.

"Don't get too cocky there, cowboy," replied Mama. "Mind tricks can appear in other unexpected places too." Young Yogi frowned. He thought he had everything figured out. There was more?

[1.9] "Like where else, Mama?" he asked.

"Well, your imagination is a good one. And although the mind tricks there can seem real, they're made out of thin air—out of nothing you can actually touch or see." Young Yogi looked up at his mom, puzzled by the idea. Learning about the Mind Monsters was exhausting!

Sensing her son's weariness, she said, "Hey, thanks for helping me, Young Yogi. Why don't you go and play now."

"Thanks, Mama!" His face brightened, and he kissed her cheek before running toward his favorite tree, with Paco scurrying behind.

The Imaginations

Young Yogi and Paco rested on their backs on the soft grass looking at the passing clouds in the sky. "Do you see that elephant?" asked Paco, pointing with his claw.

"Yes! Do you see a race car over there?" asked Young Yogi.

"Yes!" Paco clapped. "It looks more like your mom's car though."

"I see a castle."

"I see it, too. I see it!" replied Paco. "Do you see what I see? Do you see . . . The Imaginations?"

"I see them," answered Young Yogi. They sat back and readied themselves for a great show. A camera crew emerged, then a gaggle of photographers with flashing cameras and a great crowd of spectators. A man with a toothy smile appeared in a sleek suit and shiny, slicked-back hair. He winked at the camera and adjusted his tie.

"Ladies and gentlemen, it's who you've all been waiting for," he winked again at Paco and Young Yogi. "It's my great pleasure to announce the ONE. The ONLY. The Imaginations!" An audience appeared and applauded wildly.

"Thank you, Russell," answered Marvella in a silky smooth voice. She was the elegant lead singer with a giant bouffant and red sequined gown, sandwiched between two other singers equally beautiful in glamorous dresses. They went straight into their song.

Think! sang Marvella.
Don't think! chimed the backup singers.
Think about what your head does to you!

Think!
Don't Think!
Think about what your head does to you!

They danced in unison, and Marvella continued her verse.

Mind is your imagination
Like a mad TV on every station
Thoughts will control you
Take their hold and mold you
And run you to the ground . . .

You better think!
hmmm, don't think!
Think what your head does to you!
Freedom, freedom, freedom! They reached a crescendo.

Don't think!

The crowd went wild. As The Imaginations sang, their heads and arms multiplied high into the air. Young Yogi and Paco danced and jumped and laughed and clapped with the crowd around them.

"Thank you very much," said one of Marvella's heads, her silky voice hardly out of breath from such a performance. "We're The Imaginations." The crowd was cheering and screaming loudly. "We love you. We love everyone, baby!"

[1.10] That night Young Yogi hit his pillow tired from the day but determined to stay awake and avoid another night with the Mind Monsters. Before he knew it, he was asleep, and it was deep and uneventful.

[1.11] Young Yogi surprised himself hours later when he woke up without reason. He wondered in the dark if nothing happening at all was a mind trick too. Then he began to stare at the popcorn ceiling in the moonlight. He was sure he could make out the faces of the monsters, the glimmering sharpness of their teeth, their scaly skin, weird eyeballs, and terrible odor. He shivered. It was only a memory.

"Aha!" he exclaimed and nudged the chicken. "Paco! Memory does it too! The monsters aren't here, but my memory of them makes it seem like it."

"What?" asked the chicken, rubbing his eyes. "There's no monsters, Yogi. Go back to sleep."

"That's what I just said!" replied Young Yogi. Paco was snoring once again.

Surf's Up (and Down)

It was Saturday morning, Young Yogi's favorite day of the week. Time to surf! He was out the door first-thing and off to the beach when all of a sudden a rock hit him in the head. It smarted! He couldn't tell where it came from. He looked around feeling the knot form on his forehead.

"Well, well, well," said a menacing voice from the bushes.

Bharat. Young Yogi's heart sank as the knot in his forehead fell into his throat. "Looks like *baby* Yogi wants to surf! Do you even know how to *swim*?"

"Bharat, I'm just trying to get to the beach. Please just leave me alone." He could see the oversized bully clearly now from behind the bushes, and he wasn't alone.

"Let's get him!" hollered Bharat gesturing to his two smaller friends. They began to throw a storm of crab apples at him. Young Yogi tried to dodge them with his surfboard and tripped himself. Getting up with skinned knees, he ran away as fast as he could.

"That's it! Run, you chicken. Just like your stuffed doll, Paco!" The boys laughed, kicking some trash cans over as they watched Young Yogi scurry off.

Young Yogi caught his breath near the beach when he realized he wasn't being chased. He was relieved to see Anders in the distance as the sun rose high over the waves.

"Hey, little dude, c'mon!" Anders yelled, waving to Young Yogi as he ran across the sand. Anders had golden skin, blond locks of hair, and only ever wore surfing shorts.

"Dude, there are some righteous waves today, lil' Yogi!" exclaimed Anders. "Let's get to it. Dude. What happened to you?" He eyed the frazzled boy. "You okay?"

"Sure Anders," said Young Yogi, trying to act cool. "I just didn't sleep too much cause the Mind Monsters were out to get me." He knew everyone had Mind Monsters, not everyone had a bully to contend with.

"Looks like more than Mind Monsters, dude," said Anders, raising his eyebrows. Young Yogi looked away embarrassed. Anders could tell he didn't want to talk about it.

[1.12] "Oh, right. Yeah, those monsters with their mind tricks can be tough, dude. Fer sure." Anders began waxing his board. "But you can, like totally, stop them if you want to, ya know?"

"Seriously?" asked Young Yogi. "How?"

Anders jumped up, grabbed his board, and ran toward the water. "Let's surf lil' dude. C'mon!"

They got into the water. "The best way to learn is by practice, then dude, you just have to let it go," said Anders as they waited for the waves to roll in. "It's all yours Yogi, get this one coming!" Young Yogi began to paddle. He felt the swell and popped up on his board, riding the wave close to shore before he fell.

[1.13] "Remember when you couldn't even get up?" asked Anders, laughing.

"Dude, you've come a long way just by trying over and over, totally." Anders caught the next wave and rode gracefully through the pipeline, smiling and gliding with ease, like a human porpoise.

"Whoa! That was awesome!" yelled Young Yogi. "Someday I want to ride like that."

[1.14] Anders swam up to him immediately. "You can, dude! You can! Just like, practice the right way. A lot. And for, like a really long time, and without too many breaks. You gotta be total, dude!"

Young Yogi took the next wave, and caught it briefly before losing his balance. As the session carried on, it just got worse. Try as he might, he felt like a ragdoll getting battered by the currents. Then a giant wave swelled, Young Yogi began to paddle as fast as he could, and was swallowed instantly by the force of the ocean. He came up shaken and mad, and slapped the water in frustration.

"Chill out, lil' man! You've got the eagerness, but check the 'tude, dude. Stay positive no matter what!" Young Yogi tried again. And again. And again. He was waterlogged and tired, and the salt stung his wounded knees. Everyone was catching waves but him. He'd had enough.

They floated into shore. How could he suddenly hate something he loved so much? It was the worst Saturday ever. They rested on the shore, snacking on apples and watching the water. Young Yogi was unusually quiet.

[1.15] "Wanna know somethin' else?" asked Anders, breaking the silence.

"Sure," said Young Yogi, crunching miserably on his apple.

"Try to not to want stuff too much," Anders said, eating half his apple in one bite. "Like whether it's real like a wave or a toy or somethin', or like a hot babe."

Young Yogi brightened thinking of his dream bike, the Garuda 9000, with its magic bell, rickshaw driver's horn, and shiny red seat. Anders was thinking of Bette Sharma.

"It's a drag, isn't it?" questioned Anders. "Not getting what you think you want, huh? But if you get over wanting stuff, there'd be, like, nothing to be sad about, right? Got it, lil' dude?" They both snapped out of their daydreams and laughed. Young Yogi felt a little bit better.

[1.16] "Being free, dude, is not wanting anything at all, like anything," said Anders.

"That seems nearly impossible," sighed Yogi. He got up and put on his t-shirt, getting ready to go. Anders was rubbing zinc on his nose.

"Lil' Yogi," he said, "these are like directions, ya know? Not like rules or anything like that. They're just like, to show you the way, little man."

"Thanks Anders," said Young Yogi. "I'll see you later." He grabbed his board and headed toward home without the usual spring in his step.

"Be total, dude! Be total!" yelled Anders as he watched Young Yogi become a speck in the distance.

The Magic Meadow

Young Yogi decided to take a different way home hoping to avoid Bharat. He kept replaying the day in his head. Why didn't he stand up to the bullies? He could've whacked them all with his surfboard! Why couldn't he get up on his board after all those tries? He knew he could do it! Why was he so scared all the time? Lost in his thoughts, Young Yogi suddenly didn't recognize where he was.

He must have taken a wrong turn. He looked around and realized there was no turning back. The path behind him was gone! He found himself amidst wide-open green hills blanketed in brightly colored flowers. He had never seen such a place before. He came upon a cow sitting silently under a tree, her legs crossed in lotus, just like his father. She didn't look like any cow he had ever seen before. She had beautifully painted horns and mounds of flowers and beads around her neck. And she smelled good, not like other cows.

[1.17] "Hello, there," said Young Yogi politely. "Can you tell me where I am?"

"Why, the Magic Meadow, of course," said the Holy Cow with a serene smile.

"What are you doing here?" he asked, mesmerized by the cow.

"Seeking the seed inside." Young Yogi looked baffled.

"I call it the Seed-To-Be!" she continued. "Everyone's got it. Most just don't know it."

Young Yogi didn't really understand the cow, but noticed he began to feel more relaxed and happy as he listened to her.

"The seed is the key to everything," she continued, her voice as smooth as Marvella's of The Imaginations. It soothed him.

"What do you mean there's a *seed* inside us?" he asked perplexed.

"Like an acorn grows into a tree," she answered, "the tree is already there in the seed. It's already a tree, it was always a tree, and it will forever be a tree." Young Yogi looked around, everything was still and peaceful, and quite beautiful.

She changed the subject. "Young Yogi, do you see any Mind Monsters here?" How did she know his name?

"No," he answered, feeling his curiosity grow. He couldn't believe this strange cow knew about the Mind Monsters, too.

"Precisely!" she exclaimed. "There are certainly no Mind Monsters in my Magic Meadow! And there are definitely no mind tricks playing in this head!" She pointed to her skull with a brightly colored hoof.

"Even though my mind is there," she added, after a few quiet moments.

Amazing! It dawned on Young Yogi for the first time ever that it was possible to have a mind without any Mind Monsters. His own troubled thoughts seemed to be fading away. Finally, something that made sense!

"Wow!" gasped Young Yogi. The knot on his forehead didn't hurt anymore, and the scrapes on his knees had disappeared. He was beginning to enjoy this place.

"Take this seed," directed the cow. "Plant it in the ground and see for yourself." Young Yogi planted the seed and sat upon it. Soon he felt a wave of calm overtake him. His worries over the Mind Monsters stopped. They just went away! The worst Saturday ever vanished. Bharat was gone. In fact, he had no fears at all. His surfing failures didn't exist. Even his dreamy Garuda 9000 disappeared, and it didn't matter! He knew his mind was there. He could feel it, but it was like a machine that just quit working.

He sat contented and still on the mound of dirt. Suddenly, the ground beneath him began to stir. The seed sprouted abruptly, sending Young Yogi into the air! Soon he towered high above the ground as the sprout grew into a vine, twisting its tendrils around Young Yogi as it blossomed large fragrant flowers and prickly thorns. Young Yogi held out his hand and watched as the rapidly growing plant wrapped its way around his arm, taking him over. Young Yogi became part of the plant as it shot up into the sky.

[1.17] He couldn't explain what was happening; the plant began talking to him but without any words! *These flowers are your thoughts, their thorns your worries and fears.* He understood. Plant mind was like his mind. The flowers and thorns were just a *part* of the plant, naturally. Now that made sense! But there was something more. Young Yogi could smell it.

The most beautiful fragrance arose, and it carried Young Yogi more deeply inside the plant's body. He was enveloped by the scent and expanding at the same time. *The smell is part of us.* He couldn't see or touch the smell, but it was there all the same.

Suddenly, the blossoms began to shrivel, and the thorns snapped off like dry toast, leaving gleaming light in their place. Once Young Yogi gazed at the golden light, he sensed something much greater, like *he* was part of the light.

The Holy Cow looked on, sitting upon a cloud, and Young Yogi found it difficult to speak. "Everything's disappeared! Everything that seemed so real. And . . . and, I feel so happy! And I'm a part of everything. And everything is part of me." His head bobbled from the top of the towering vine.

Chewing her cud and filing her hoof with a nail file, the cow said, "Just don't mistake that for the end of the story, Young Yogi." The vine grew upward one last time, sending Young Yogi's head above the clouds. He entered a place where there were no questions and no answers. In fact, everything was so clear there was no need of them. He understood *everything*. Perfectly. He had never experienced that before. The Seed-To-Be.

[1.18] The Holy Cow's head popped above the clouds, and she asked a very peculiar question, "Do you like movies?"

"Uh, sure," said Young Yogi, surprised at the sound of his own voice. He liked this place high above the clouds and thought to himself that it felt like a big empty space that held everything.

"It is!" replied the cow. "It *is* a big empty space that holds everything." How could the cow hear his unspoken words?

"Yes, I can hear your silent thoughts," she answered aloud. *How could something so empty feel so full?* He thought.

"Because," she replied, "this place is like . . . a giant endless movie screen! And me? I just love my moooovies!"

She projected herself into the empty space first wearing a big ball gown, batting her long eyelashes behind a lace fan with pin curls in her hair. As Young Yogi watched, he realized his life was just like a movie too. He was like a character on a screen. Then the cow morphed herself into a spacesuit and floated around Young Yogi's head. "Houston, we have a problem!"

Young Yogi had to join in! He projected himself right into a spaceship and zoomed around the cow and off into the distance.

Then the Holy Cow galloped up to him on a horse and tipped her cowboy hat. "Howdy partner. This is what the Seed-To-Be is like, I reckon," she said gesturing to the blank space.

"As endless and amazing as this empty space that has everything at the same time?" asked Yogi, scaling a wall like his favorite superhero.

"Yep, you betcha."

They sat atop the highest cloud looking up, returning to their normal selves. The Holy Cow asked another question, "Do you like games?"

"Yes!" answered Young Yogi. He loved games.

"Seeking the Seed-To-Be is like a game. It seems to be hidden from our view, but all we have to do is remember it's there. And because we always forget, we always get to re-remember. It's a great game!"

[1.19] They lowered through the clouds. "Some people don't need to play the game at all. They are born knowing, and they never ever forget the Seed-To-Be that's inside them." Just then Young Yogi's Great-Great-Grandpapa Yoga-ji appeared from the light, walking with his stick with a little dog at his side.

"Yes," said the Holy Cow, "your Great-Great-Grandpapa Yoga-ji was indeed such a fellow."

"I remember Nana Yogini telling me stories about him," recalled Young Yogi, finding it easier to speak now. "He used to sit for months at a time without moving. Bugs were even crawling all over him! Nothing seemed to bother him."

[1.20] The Holy Cow continued, "The rest of us aren't born so lucky. We have to try a lot, lot harder. We have to believe we can do it, with all our might and focus with all our whole heart." They were back through the clouds now.

"Don't forget that the magic Seed-To-Be is inside everyone and everything," added Great-Great-Grandpapa Yoga-ji, patting the dog's head affectionately and waving good-bye.

"That seems like a whole lot of work," said Young Yogi, starting to feel like his doubtful, fearful old self again. The blinding light in the meadow was softening. They were back down on the ground now.

[1.21] "Not for those who are keen!" said the Holy Cow. "Just take a look at my garden!" She pointed to her lush and tidy vegetable garden.

[1.22] "Like these chilies here, there are mild ones, medium ones, and set-your-cud-on-fire-HOT!" The chilies perked up, and two opened their eyes. One was sleepy, one was normal, and one was already wide awake and vibrant.

"Now if these chilies had a Seed-To-Be race, who do you think would get there quicker?" asked the Holy Cow crossing her hooves over her chest. Young Yogi looked at the garden; he couldn't believe the cow had a fondness for chilies.

"Uh, well—" he started.

"That's right!" exclaimed the cow, gesturing to the flame-colored perky pepper. "This baby here is burning with intensity! It's so focused on being a hot pepper, you better believe it'll get there quicker!"

The cow plucked the hottest pepper and started salivating. Young Yogi wasn't quite getting the point and only said, "Geeze, I didn't know cows even liked chilies." She took a bite.

"Whoooo-wheeee!" she mooed. "Hot dang!" The spice sent the cow spinning right into the sky again, past the clouds and back into that big empty-everything space before she came spinning back down and landed in front of Young Yogi.

She offered him a bite. "Well, Yogi, if chilies aren't quite your thing, you could always try something else." Young Yogi refused the chili, shaking his hands. She munched thoughtfully on the rest of the pepper like it was a carrot. This cow was crazy!

"No thanks, Holy Cow. I don't really like spicy things. What else did you have in mind?"

[1.23] "You could always try letting go completely," she said, picking at her teeth with a toothpick.

"Letting go of what exactly?" asked Young Yogi. He began to wonder if he could keep up with the Holy Cow as she told him all these new things.

She was speaking a mile a minute now from the hot chili, "The infinite invisible invincible sensational supreme source huge humongous happening vast valiant visionary aligned absolute absorption real rockin' reality amazing awareness ally." She took a big breath finally.

[1.24] "Or, I.S.H.V.A.R.A. For short." She sat back now under a leafy tree. She was ready to relax.

"I.S.H.V.A.R.A. runs all things, beats our hearts, blows the wind, shines the sun. It's like a cosmic clock with no hands. And is beyond the things which make us suffer."

[1.25] Young Yogi lay beside the Holy Cow as they looked up at the sky. "I.S.H.V.A.R.A. knows everything and has no beginning and no end!" the cow continued. "It's like an all-seeing invisible eye in the sky. Only I.S.H.V.A.R.A. is everywhere and also in you!"

Everything suddenly seemed brighter and clearer to Young Yogi, as if he had just dusted off his eyeballs.

[1.26] The Holy Cow said, "I.S.H.V.A.R.A. is the teacher of all teachers."

"Even of Mr. Siva?" asked Young Yogi, thinking of his teacher, the smartest person he knew.

"The teacher of ALL!" bellowed the cow.

A faint sound emerged and then became louder. "Ommm, Ommm, Ommm!" echoed in their ears.

"What's that beautiful sound?" asked Young Yogi. Suddenly a large flock of rainbow-colored birds appeared in the sky.

"Why, those are the Ommmingales, of course," said the Holy Cow. Hundreds of birds appeared now. The largest of the birds landed on the cow's head and chirped in her ear.

"I was just getting to that," said the cow to the bird.

[1.27/1.28] "He said that is the sound of I.S.H.V.A.R.A., and you should repeat it and think upon it as often as you can," interpreted the cow. Young Yogi and the Holy Cow joined the bird chorus and the sweet symphony of sound.

"Ooooooooooooooooommmmmmmmmmm . . . "

[1.29] Young Yogi was tranquil, his mind clear of all thoughts and troubles. He felt larger than his body, like he was part of the sound itself.

A bird tweeted in his ear, "The magic word will always keep the Mind Monsters away," and flitted into the sky. Young Yogi felt so grateful. It was a new feeling for him to be so peaceful and connected.

"Thank you Ommmingales! Thank you Holy Cow! Thank you Magic Meadow! Thank you Great-Great-Grandpapa Yoga-ji! Thank you Seed-To-Be! Thank you I.S.H.V.A.R.A.!"

They ommmed into the setting sun.

The Worst Day Ever

"How did you sleep?" asked Papa Yogi the next morning as he placed some fresh idlis on Young Yogi's plate.

"No Mind Monsters came last night, Papa!" he said proudly, biting into a steamy rice cake. "Now that I know about who I am from the Seed-To-Be and the magic word Om!"

"That's great, Yogi," he replied. "You must have met the Holy Cow."

"You know the Holy Cow?" asked Young Yogi, surprised.

"She's a good friend of mine. We go way back, from my beach days in Goa." Young Yogi lingered cheerfully over his food.

"Now finish up your breakfast, and I'll drop you at school. We're running late today," said Papa, grabbing his helmet.

They zoomed through the streets on an old but zippy scooter. Papa Yogi continued, "You know Yogi, I know you had a great experience in the Magic Meadow. There's no better place to go to remember who you are! So I hate to bring this up, but the path of a yogi never stops." Papa waited a few moments to let it sink in, he knew it was difficult.

"There's more you need to know about the Mind Monsters." Young Yogi was feeling so good from the Meadow, from a restful night's sleep, and enjoying the wind blowing on his face riding on the back of the scooter. It was hard to believe what his father was saying.

"There's more to them than just their mind tricks," he said, pulling up to a stoplight. A cloud of exhaust began to grow around them. Young Yogi was quickly annoyed in his disappointment. The light changed, and Papa Yogi dodged a rickshaw, "There are things that make it easier for the Mind Monsters to come in the first place."

"Really?" asked Young Yogi, skeptically. He thought he had all the answers he needed. Everything seemed so clear in the Magic Meadow. He was connected to everything! Why was his dad trying to ruin it? He held tightly to his father as they weaved through a herd of goats on the road. His heart began to sink.

"I can't take it anymore!" His dad looked back surprised. "Every time I think I've got it figured out, there's always something else!" Young Yogi scowled. They pulled up in front of the school.

"Sorry, son," said Papa, "I know it's not easy. A yogi's path is full of challenges. But don't give up. You might even be surprised where this all takes you." Young Yogi rolled his eyes. "Now, you certainly don't want to be late for Mr. Siva's class!" Young Yogi was so frustrated he stormed off the scooter without saying good-bye.

"Listen up!" bellowed Mr. Siva, tapping the chalkboard boldly with his pointer. "Today we look at what attracts the Mind Monsters, like BEES to a HONEY-POT."

Mr. Siva had a voice so deep and stern it shook the walls. He wore glasses, thick and dirty as buttered toast. "You want Mind Monsters? Just be sure to leave *this* trail of BREADCRUMBS, and they'll follow you straight away!"

The class opened their notebooks with trembling hands. "Today's lecture is on the Monster MAGNETS. You may not have heard of them before, but I guarantee you know what they are!" He made a dramatic pause.

[1.30] "There are NINE Monster Magnets. They are: Being SICK! DULL! DOUBTFUL! CARELESS! LAZY! CRAVING! MAKE-BELIEVE! MISSING THE POINT! GOING BACKWARD!"

The students all wrote frantically trying to keep up, except for Bharat who sat smugly in the back.

"Now these magnets INVITE the Monsters right into your head," continued Mr. Siva. "You might as well roll out the RED CARPET for them!"

The class was uneasy, though whether it was from the information or Mr. Siva himself was hard to say. One brave student, Marlon, raised his hand. "Uh, 'em, Mr. Siva could you please, uh, repeat that, sir?"

"The Mind Monsters are already knocking on *your* door with your laziness!" he replied.

Bharat finally opened his notebook, tore out a piece of paper, shoved it in his mouth, and began chewing it slowly. He eyed Young Yogi a few chairs over.

Mr. Siva continued, "When you are ILL!" He looked at Maria blowing her nose.

"When you space OUT!" he said, startling poor Clive who was staring out the window.

"When you have DOUBTS! You know what those are!" Mr. Siva looked out at the whole troubled class.

Meanwhile, Bharat took out the spit wad from his mouth and pulled a straw out from under his desk. He aimed the giant spitball right for Young Yogi's head.

Mr. Siva didn't seem to notice and continued, "When you don't give your FULL attention to the TASK at hand!" Everyone else's eyes were glued to Mr. Siva, their hands speeding along their notebooks. "We've covered laziness, haven't we class?" He adjusted his thick glasses on his nose.

"Yes, Mr. Siva!" they answered in careful unison. Bharat held his aim like a sniper while Mr. Siva continued to speak.

"Where was I?" he paused. "When you want this thing and that thing! Like a Garuda 9000!" He looked at Young Yogi squarely in the eyes. "You think that'll make you happy?" Young Yogi shifted nervously in his seat.

Just then, the second Mr. Siva left Young Yogi's desk, a flying wet spitball splatted into Yogi's face, sliming down his cheek. Bharat gave a menacing smile.

Mr. Siva didn't notice, "Or when you live in the little land of MAKE-BELIEVE!" With a huff, he picked up Harriet's notebook with her drawings of unicorns, monster-repellent fairies, and magic meadows.

"Or, when you COMPLETELY miss the point! Is anyone paying attention at all?"

"Yes, Mr. Siva!" they stammered.

Young Yogi wiped his cheek. There was no escaping Bharat. That was quite literally, the last straw! Young Yogi had had enough. He took his eraser, the only thing he had, and lobbed it as hard as he could at Bharat.

Mr. Siva carried on, "Then don't take ONE step forward and TWO steps back, and get STUCK there!" The teacher was oblivious. "Mind Monsters call that the CHA-CHA! You want to dance the cha-cha, hmm?"

The eraser missed its mark, and Bharat smirked.

"Furthermore!" The room rumbled with his words. "The Monsters *love* your pain and despair." Mr. Siva paused.

"Mr. Bharat! Mr. Young Yogi!" The class turned to stare at them. Young Yogi was petrified, and Bharat rolled his eyes. "You are FODDER for the Mind Monsters! Do NOT interrupt my lecture." He slammed his pointer on his desk. There was an unusually long silence before he spoke again. He pushed his glasses on his nose.

[1.31] "Where was I? That's right—misery. Pain and despair." He cleared his throat. "There are signs that the Magnets have taken effect. The more miserable you are, the better! Shaking? Can't breathe because you're so upset? Talk about flashing NEON lights! You just gave the Mind Monsters FREE passes to your sad show!"

Mr. Siva looked straight at the two boys. Young Yogi felt his heart race and his palms sweat. His breath was short as he trembled in his seat. He'd never be free of the Mind Monsters.

"Got 'em all? That's the 'Monster Express' delivery right to your door!"

I'm doomed, thought Young Yogi. He had every symptom in the book.

"Now, learn these for tomorrow's test. Mind Monsters will be in attendance to see how well you remember." The bell rang. "Class dismissed!"

A test!

The class scurried out the door, except for Bharat and Young Yogi, who were hooked by their belt loops with Mr. Siva's long pointer. After an uncomfortable silence, he shook his head in disappointment. Beads of sweat formed on Yogi's brow, and even Bharat gulped. They waited. Mr. Siva said only three words: "After. School. Detention."

Young Yogi walked down the hall forlorn. With his head spinning and aching, he was a walking Monster Magnet. Bharat was on his case and now *detention*. The cherry on top of this monster of a mess—Mr. Siva's impossible test! Panic set in.

He needed a drink.

"Hey, Young Yogi," greeted Guru, the coconut man, in a soft voice. "You look like you could use a coconut." He handed the frazzled boy a fresh one.

"How will I ever get these monsters off my back?" asked Young Yogi. "There's all those monsters, their tricks. And Magnets too! I'll never be able to keep it all straight." He sighed and slurped the sweet coconut water, about to mention his detention problem, when Guru spoke.

[1.32] "Do what I do." He took a large coconut in his hands and with a single whack of his giant knife, cracked it evenly in two. "Focus on a single point." He handed Young Yogi some fresh coconut meat. Young Yogi never got tired of seeing Guru's skill and managed a smile.

Guru continued with a gleam in his eye, "With too many distractions, how is anyone meant to do anything? One thing at a time, Young Yogi. Step-by-step."

He grabbed another coconut and cracked the top.

"Here, have another coconut. On the house."

The last bell of the day rang, which was usually Young Yogi's favorite sound of the day. But not today, which was sure to be the worst day ever. He felt heavy as he gathered his belongings. Paco stuck his head out of the backpack.

"C'mon Yogi. It's not so bad. You stood up to Bharat. I mean, kind of . . . " His voice drifted. "You *could* work on your aim, you know." His attempt to cheer Yogi was failing.

"Gee, thanks," replied Young Yogi, slumbering down the hall.

"Bharat's not *that* scary. Big, yes. But scary, not so much."

"It's easy for you to say, all you have to do is act like a stuffed animal."

"I resent that!" exclaimed the chicken.

The sign posted on the detention room door interrupted them. It read: "Banyan Forest Clean-Up Duty Now!"

"What?" cried Young Yogi. "You've got to be kidding me."

"Great. Just great." said Paco. This *was* the worst day ever.

In the Banyans

They walked out to the forest behind the school, still bickering. Bharat was already there waiting. Paco went limp. "Where's everyone else?" asked Young Yogi, suspicious.

"How should I know?" replied Bharat. "There's only these bags and brooms and stuff. No one's here. Why should I do anything? I wouldn't even be here if it wasn't for you."

"Are you serious?" asked Young Yogi. His blood boiled. Normally, he cowered when speaking to Bharat, but it had been a long day. He was fed up! "You started it. You started all of this!"

"What are you gonna do, Yogi? Tell your only friend, Paco? A *doll?*" asked Bharat, egging him on.

Young Yogi charged Bharat, catching him off guard and knocking him over.

"That's it, Yogi," called Paco. "C'mon!" He shadowboxed from the side with bright red boxing gloves on his claws, cheering him on.

The boys rolled, kicked, and punched in a flurry on the forest floor. They created a cyclone of dust in which they could not see anything, or notice that they were being coiled upward in the long tendrils of a great banyan tree. Any lessons Young Yogi had learned about taming the monsters in his mind were taken over by an intense rage. He couldn't see Bharat anymore yet continued to hit and kick the air as if he were fighting all alone against the world.

"Naughty, naughty!" said a gruff voice. The dust began to settle, and the boys saw that they were suspended in the air, wrapped up amidst the thousands of thin vines and twisted branches of a huge gnarly tree. The great banyan towered so far and wide, Young Yogi could only see leaves and branches all around them. Although it looked as if there were many separate trees in this infinite forest, they were all joined to this giant one that held them now.

"Naughty, naughty," the great banyan said again. The boys looked at each other, panting and frightened. Their clothes in tatters, their skin covered in dusty scrapes. Hanging limply in the air, they nearly became allies in this strange and dark place.

"Uh, fellas," stammered Paco. "Did you hear that?" He was wrapped in tendrils down below.

Bharat couldn't believe it. The chicken talked!

The Banyan spoke again. "Naughty boys. Tsk. Tsk. Not everyone visits the great banyan forest. And of those who do, well, not everyone gets out." The tree's voice seemed to change from gruff to something more, well musical. It had a strange

accent, what was it? The tree ruffled its leaves.

"O'Banyan's the name, and this is my forest, so it is."

Irish, was the tree Irish?

"Look, tree," said Bharat, returning to his old self, "let me down! Like I said, I wouldn't even be here if it wasn't for that Young Yogi." He directed his head toward the boy hanging across from him.

Young Yogi immediately responded, "Now hold on a minute! Bharat started it! He's been picking on me for months!"

Paco chimed in, "I didn't even do anything!" The three were stunned into silence when the tree tightened its twiny vines around them.

[1.33] "That'll do lads, that'll do, so it will," replied the tree. "Now yas need to listen and listen up good, so you do. Take a look around yas with yer eyes." The forest came to life before them. All the different branches had their own personalities, some nice, some cruel, some grumpy, some sad. Some argued and fought like the boys, some hugged and danced, some twirled around and got sick while others slept or cried.

"How does 'ol O'Banyan handle this moody lot, yas might ask yeselves?" Young Yogi, Paco, and Bharat were mesmerized by the scene. How could *trees* have all these emotions and do all these things?

"Simple!" continued the tree. "Kindness. Plain 'ol-fashioned kindness." The tree began to ease his grip of the three. "See here, I loves 'em all, so I do. With all their foibles and such. Whether they're happy or sad or whatnot makes no difference to me. 'Tis not my business 'atall, so it isn't. I likes 'em all just the same."

"Doesn't it drive you crazy?" asked Young Yogi.

"Crazy is letting it get to ye," said the tree. "I'd rather have me piece of mind, thank ye very much."

O'Banyan lit up, and the whole forest was illuminated. For as far as their eyes could see, there was only forest—endless trees, vines, and branches connected together in every direction.

"See that?" asked the tree.

"You're all attached together!" said Young Yogi.

"Yeah, they're all coming from you!" said Bharat, authentically excited.

"The whole forest is you!" exclaimed Paco.

"Good on ye, lads," said O'Banyan. "There's hope for yas yet, so there is."

Bharat began to feel, well, different somehow. It seemed weird to say, but he felt like he was linked to the tree, in a strange way. And, maybe to everything else, even Young Yogi. Such an odd feeling felt foreign to him, but also, really good!

The tree began to lower them down to the ground. Seeing the truth of the forest as the tendrils loosened around them, brought a peace to the boys and erased their pasts together almost instantly. Until now, they didn't realize they were connected too.

"Young Yogi, I'm sorry," Bharat found himself saying. He had never said those words before to anyone. "I've really been a jerk!" Inside he understood why he had been so mean all the time. He had been afraid.

Bharat's change of heart surprised Young Yogi. He realized he had never really seen the boy before him. Bharat was only, ever, a monster and a bully, made up in his mind and firmly believed. Things were not what they seemed!

"It's okay," said Yogi, touched by his courage, "I haven't been so nice either." Paco was swinging on one of the vines, looking on.

Bharat said, "And I'm sorry to you too, Paco. I mean, I really did think you were a stuffed animal."

"People always think that," said the chicken. "I'm used to it."

The tree shook and said, "Lads, hate to interrupt this peace treaty, but yas should know there's magic of sorts in this here forest, so there is. It may or may not suit yas, that's dependin'."

"Depending on what?" asked Young Yogi.

"Depends if yas want to stay here forevers or not." The boys looked at each other. The forest seemed nice and all, but they didn't want to leave Coconut Grove.

"If that's the case then, yas should be gettin' a move on, so you should. Yas need to get out of the forest by sunrise, or that's it!"

"Well, Mr. O'Banyan," said Bharat, "can you help us get out of here?" The sun was beginning to set in the forest. The tree was beginning to seem, well more like a *tree*. Still and quiet. The forest also settled and appeared as it did when they first arrived. Everything had gone so quiet.

"Mr. O'Banyan?" asked Young Yogi. Paco gently pecked at O'Banyan's trunk.

"Mr. O'Banyan?" asked Bharat. "You still there?"

Silence.

"I guess he's gone now," said Yogi.

"What're we gonna do?" asked Bharat. "How do we get out of here?"

The tree stirred and managed to point with one of its long vines in a northeasterly direction.

"I guess we head that way," said Young Yogi. "Thanks, O'Banyan!"

Chai 'n Chats

They walked through the dim forest together, heading in the general direction pointed out by O'Banyan. It was dark and difficult to see, so they didn't realize they were no longer walking on the ground. Somewhere along the way, the three walked up a windy tree limb, elevating them into a sky-high system of branchy, tangled pathways. They were lost in conversation.

"I've never told anyone this, you guys," said Bharat, "but my dad never escaped from a Mind Maze. He was fooled big time by the Mind Monsters. He couldn't get out. I guess he wasn't a very good yogi." Young Yogi and Paco looked at him in shock, then tenderness.

"I'm really afraid of them!" he continued. "Of the Mind Monsters, ya know?" Bharat surprised himself by opening up. He'd never done that before either.

"Me too!" said Young Yogi, who then told him all about his nightmares and his experience with the Holy Cow in the Magic Meadow.

As the boys chatted away, Paco was pecking around for food when he finally realized they were up in the air. "Fellas," he squawked, "we're really lost! I mean we're not even on the ground anymore."

"Uh-oh," Young Yogi replied, "yeah, you're right." They stopped to have a look in amazement.

"Well, now we have a bird's-eye view, eh Paco?" Bharat nudged the chicken.

Once the joking and chatter settled, they remembered the gravity of their situation. Then, someone's stomach grumbled loudly. "I'm so hungry!" said Bharat, "Aren't you guys? Mmmm, pizza, lasagna, dosas, oh, and burritos and onion bhaji with—"

"Bharat!" interrupted Young Yogi. "You gotta stop all this talk about food. It's making me crazy."

"I'm starving too," said Paco, "but don't you think we should try to figure out where we are?"

They surveyed the branchy horizon. They could just make out the endless maze of gnarled branches and bushy leaves in the darkness, and not much else.

"Maybe we should just wait until morning when we can see," said Bharat.

"We can't," said Yogi. "Remember what O'Banyan said? If we ever want to see home again, we've got to get of here before that!"

"Guys, look!" jumped Paco, pointing in the distance with his claw. "I think there's some light over there. See it?"

"Yeah! Good eye, bird," said Bharat.

"Let's head that way. Maybe we can get some help," said Young Yogi.

It's impossible to say just how long it took them to get to that beacon of light. It was like being near the summit of a mountain, so close and yet so far. They walked and dropped and climbed and swung their way through the knotted treetops. Finally, the light was really ahead of them.

"I can't believe it," shouted Bharat, sprinting ahead with new-found energy, toward a clearing on a giant limb.

"Joy House," Young Yogi read the sign aloud, seeing of all things, a chai stand, perched comfortably on the widest of branches.

"I can't believe it!" Bharat said again, "Chai! And bikkies!" Even Paco rushed over pecking at the crumbs near the stall. There were three interesting looking fellows there.

Chai Wallah, a tea master extraordinaire, was mixing a secret recipe of spices, tea, and milk in high streams over his head. Sadhu Sam was sitting down with one leg behind his head, sipping a cup of hot tea. Young Yogi wondered how he got his leg around such a big mound of hair. And, Snake Charmer played his flute near a big basket. There were some scruffy, but cute, street dogs laying around. It was a lazy and comfortable place.

"Two chai please! Oh, I mean three. Sorry, Paco," said Bharat. "And some biscuits too, please." Chai Wallah nodded with a bright smile. The three didn't realize how tired they were until they sat down. Once they had some chai and biscuits, Bharat broke the silence.

"You know, stuck out here in the banyans has me really thinking," said Bharat. "I mean, what if I'm just like my dad. What if I get stuck like him? Stuck in a

Mind Monster web I can never get out of? Or, stuck here forever and never go home?"

"You're not your father," said Young Yogi. "We got to remember, we're not our minds!" The Mind Monsters would generate their thoughts, but he didn't have to *believe* in any of them. Young Yogi felt clearer in the banyans.

"And, we'll find a way home," said Paco.

"I don't know about you guys, but my Mind Monsters are really strong!" said Bharat, chomping on another biscuit.

[1.34] "Mind Monsterssssssssssss?" interrupted a snake, lifting its head out of the basket next to the boys. They looked over at the large cobra and sipped nervously at their tea.

"Uh, yeah," Bharat stammered, "what do you know about Mind Monsters, m-Mr. Snake?"

Shyam left the basket and slithered around the boys. "Look at my masssssssster. Ssssssee him!" The snake gestured with his hood toward the Snake Charmer seated beside them.

"Ssssssee him!" repeated Shyam as he slithered near the man's belly. "Lisssssten." The boys stared at the Snake Charmer breathing in and out very, very slowly.

"He breathessssss," said the snake, "ssssssee, lisssssssten." They all watched entranced. "He inhalessssss," and after a minute the snake continued, "he exhalessssss."

"He holds his breath too!" said Young Yogi.

"Cool," said Bharat, "but what does that have to do with Mind Monsters?"

"He controlsssss the breathssssss," replied Shyam. "No monssssssterssss, sssssee?"

"Uh," said Bharat, "you just *watch* your breath? That seems too simple." He was in disbelief.

"Ssssssimple not sssssso ssssssssimple." The Snake Charmer stopped his breathing and took a sip of chai. The snake slithered onto his lap, nodding contentedly at the boys and Paco.

"No Mind Monsters bother me," said Snake Charmer in a calm voice.

[1.35] Chai Wallah chimed in behind his steaming pots of tea. "Well . . . what I do . . ."

They all watched the streams of chai pass over his head from cup to cup, like a rainbow. "I, I, I focus on the chai, chai, chai!" His eyes locked to his task with no chance of distraction. "No Mind Monsters bother me either," he added.

"That's because his whole mind is focused on one thing, one thing only," said Sadhu Sam, Chai Wallah's brother. "I taught him that. He's my little brother after all." He put his other leg behind his head and gulped his chai. His coiled matted hair made him two feet taller.

[1.36] "Me?" said Sadhu Sam between sips of tea, "I don't need to focus on something on the outside to fend off the Mind Monsters. I have what you might call my own portable inner light. It's like the best technology!"

"Yeah," said Chai Wallah, "he's developed that light through years of yogic training. Keeps him free of any sorrows."

"No sssssssorrowsssssss," repeated the snake curling up into its basket. Sadhu Sam sat quietly, after some moments his inner light appeared above his brow, so they could all see it. He sat very still for a long time.

[1.37] Finally, when he came back, Sadhu Sam said, "So you see, you can use just about anything to focus upon as long as it doesn't create more desire inside you."

"Um, so I guess the Garuda 9000 wouldn't work then?" asked Young Yogi disappointed.

"Or gulab jamuns," added Bharat, thinking of the syrupy sweets he loved so much.

"Actually, they'd be the perfect objects for you if they *didn't* create any wanting," added Snake Charmer. "Practically anything will do."

[1.38] The scruffiest of street dogs, Clover, woke up from her slumber and said, wagging her tail, "I like to use what I learn from my sleep and dreams." Chai Wallah fed her a biscuit, and Bharat pet her chin. He just made a friend for life. "No Mind Monsters get me either."

With all the chat at the chai stand, they forgot why they came there in the first place and that they wanted to get home! "It's really nice here, and the chai is great–" said Young Yogi.

"But we need to find our way back to Coconut Grove," finished Bharat.

"Before we can never get back!" added Paco.

The chai gang looked at each other. "Don't you see?" asked Sadhu Sam. "You could be like us. Mind Monster-free. And in no need of a home to be at peace."

"And you could work here if you wanted," said Chai Wallah. They all looked at each other. It was tempting, but they all knew in that moment the choice was made.

"Can I go with you?" asked Clover, the dog.

"You bet!" said Bharat, rubbing her ears.

"The thing is, boys," said Sadhu Sam, "you've got to do it now or it'll be too late!"

"If you stay here too long without taming the mind," said Snake Charmer.

"The Monssssstersssss will get you for good!" continued Shyam, the snake.

"That must've been what O'Banyan was trying to tell us," said Young Yogi.

Suddenly they could hear a rumbling in the trees, like they were being torn down. In fact, they were! The forest was being demolished by the sharp fangs and slime of a giant Mind Monster in the distance.

"You've got everything you need," said Chai Wallah.

"But, you must go now!" said Snake Charmer.

"We've got to get out of here!" said Bharat, scrambling to get up with Clover at his heels.

"There's only one way we can go," yelled Young Yogi. He picked up Paco and started to run away from the loud chomping sounds. The chai gang waved casually, and then Joy House evaporated away like the steam from a chai pot.

Panicked, they ran as fast as they could. They were at the whims of their minds as they tried to escape and kept hitting dead ends amidst the tangled branches and having to retrace their steps, high above the ground. The chomping was getting louder, and they could hear the sharp teeth ripping into the foliage and bark.

"We're never going to get out of here," panted Paco. "Those large teeth are going to tear into my feathers and chicken belly." He began to run around frantically in circles. "This is it, I tell you!"

Young Yogi felt his adrenaline surge and his fear escalate. Maybe this *was* it. There was no escape. He *was* weak and afraid. They ran into another dead end!

Suddenly, Young Yogi froze.

"C'mon!" said Bharat. "We gotta keep going!"

"I'm not going," said Young Yogi.

"Are you crazy?" asked Bharat, his eyes manic with fear.

"Have we learned nothing after all of this?" he asked. He sat down. "I'm not going."

Young Yogi began chanting the sound of the Ommmingales. "Ommmmmmmmmm, Ommmmmmm . . . " It was powerful and began to calm Bharat and Paco.

"He's right," said Paco. "We're running around like headless chickens!" He began

to focus on a single leaf in front of him.

Bharat could feel the breath of the monster on the back of his neck. "Okay, I can do this. I can do this," he said psyching himself up. "Don't believe my mind. I'm *not* believing my mind. But the monster is coming." The glare from the monster's tooth was blinding him. His fearful thoughts consumed him. Young Yogi and Paco were focused and unaffected.

"His breath reeks!" shouted Bharat. The giant mouth engulfed him.

Bharat found himself hanging from the monster's epiglottis when it dawned on him. *Breathe!* He recalled Shyam's voice, "Inhalesssssss, exhalesssssssss." Bharat began to watch his breath as he swung back and forth in the monster's huge throat. He calmed down with each sway and breath. Finally, his thoughts, stories, and fears left him, and when the monster's mouth opened, Bharat swung right out of it and landed in front of Young Yogi and Paco.

"You did it!" said Young Yogi. They high-fived each other.

"We did it!" said Bharat. They watched as the forest disappeared and the last vine of the banyan tree was ingested into the monster's mouth, and then the giant, scaly beast disintegrated, leaving them back on the ground, just on the outskirts of Coconut Grove.

"Well, at least this is a place we recognize," said Young Yogi. "It's a long walk, but we're not far from home now." In the dawn's light, they walked along the dusty road in a contented silence when Rickshaw Rita came zipping along.

"Hey, hey fellas!" she said. Rickshaw Rita was a two-time world champion Rickshaw Renegade driver and the fastest, most famous driver in town. "Let me give you a lift. Chai Wallah told me you were in the banyans, so I thought I'd keep an eye out for ya. It's a long walk to Coconut Grove. Glad you made it out."

"It was close," said Young Yogi.

"I was almost eaten up," exclaimed Bharat. They proceeded to recap their adventures to her.

"I'm glad to see Sadhu Sam is still around and Snake Charmer too. I used to know them back in Goa."

"Did you know the Holy Cow too?" asked Young Yogi.

"Oh, you betcha," answered Rickshaw Rita, "Me and HC used to gallivant all around the Magic Meadow, sing with the Ommmingales, seek the Seed, make our own movies up there in that big empty space. It was fantastic! I don't get out there much anymore, or the banyans either."

"Why not?" asked Bharat.

[1.39] "Don't need to really, ya know? Good places to learn a thing or two, and fun as hell, pardon my language. I 'spose I took in those lessons pretty good, and well, those monsters just love a troubled mind, don't they? But they never get to me since I can focus on whatever I want. It's my choice." She skillfully weaved through the traffic as they neared the town, dodging animals, cars, scooters, and people at a high speed.

"You mean you can use anything at all, and the monsters don't bother you?" asked Young Yogi.

"Wow!" said Bharat, impressed.

[1.40] "Yogis like us," she said, "can focus ourselves on just about anything, as you well know by now. From the tiniest grain of sand or speck of dust—hey! Watch it, buster!" She yelled at a passing truck that cut her off, and immediately finished her thought, "—to the largest. Like the sky up above or the Milky Way."

Rickshaw Rita decided to take the scenic route. She pressed a button marked "Hyper-Drive," and catapulted the rickshaw into the sky. They drove all through the Milky Way, blinded by stars before coming down and landing in front of Young Yogi's house.

"Gotta get a move on, fellas. Gotta hot date with Chai Wallah tonight," said Rickshaw Rita winking. "See ya!"

They barely had time to get out of the rickshaw, as she took off at lightning speed. "Thanks Rickshaw Rita!" they yelled waving, but she was already long gone.

Under the Water

Many days later, Young Yogi was playing in the Magic Meadow. What a week! He hadn't seen any Mind Monsters since the banyans. He had no conflicts of any kind now that he was friends with Bharat. He surfed pretty good on Saturday and even passed his test in Mr. Siva's class. It seemed all the things that caused him stress before were no longer problems. He kept remembering all the people he met who knew how to control their Mind Monsters and how they did it. And now he seemed to be doing it too. It was the longest period of time since he encountered the Mind Monsters that there were *no* Mind Monsters. He felt content and at ease. And, he began to wonder just what it would be like to be free of them once and for all.

"What would life be like with no Mind Monsters ever?" He asked himself aloud, sitting beside a glistening lake. He threw a stone in the water and watched how it disturbed the surface. Then the ripples settled, and the dirt sank to the bottom. The top was clear and still again. It did this all on its own. Young Yogi was fascinated by what he saw, the ripples were like the water's own Mind Monsters. And the water calmed itself!

[1.41] Drawn to the lake, Young Yogi stepped closer and looked into the shimmering liquid. He ran his hand through the water and realized he and his reflection and all that the water mirrored were one. He could not tell anything apart. He was part of this reflecting liquid jewel.

How did he not see this before? A calm overcame him, and the world was still. He was so mesmerized by his reflection merging into the ripples that he fell right into the water!

Paco was sitting on the shore and panicked when he saw Young Yogi sink deeper beneath the surface. "Young Yogi!" he exclaimed, shaking his feathers in a frenzy.

He didn't know what to do. Paco didn't know how to swim.

[1.42] Young Yogi sank into a beautiful, magical place. His parents appeared waving as he rode by on a brand-new shiny Garuda 9000. He saw Mr. Siva swimming with his pointer, wearing goggles and guiding a school of students along a coral reef. He pedaled past The Imaginations synchronized swimming in bright, sequined bathing suits to the beat of Guru the coconut man's coconut shell drums and the flute of the Snake Charmer, who was floating on a clam. Pascal was there too, hanging mischievously on the rear wheel of the Garuda 9000 by his tail. The Holy Cow snorkeled by in a flowered swim cap and matching suit, waving her colored hoof by some mermaids. Chai Wallah and Rickshaw Rita surfed atop her rickshaw.

Young Yogi felt so warm and happy seeing all his friends and family there together. It was the perfect place! All the Mind Monsters he had ever known were there too, swimming in a big school but not bothering anyone.

Paco watched the bubbles rise on the surface of the pond and squawked. He needed to get help and fast!

[1.43] A luminous light appeared beneath the water, and Young Yogi felt so comfortable and at peace, even though his family and friends were fading away. His Garuda 9000 morphed into a surfboard, and as he rode effortlessly toward the magnetic light, Sadhu Sam came into view, meditating with his legs behind his head. The glow from his brow merged with the emanating light around him as he slowly began to dissolve away. Young Yogi felt his body become lighter as if he may begin to dissolve too.

Meanwhile, Paco ran as fast as he could. He saw Anders eating a burrito and flirting with Bette Sharma. Anders did a double take. Was that a rubber chicken running in front of him?

"I'm not rubber!" said Paco. "Young Yogi is in trouble! I need your help!" Paco was running around in circles.

"Alright, dude, alright. Calm down," said Anders and took another bite of his bean supreme, winking at Bette. Paco pecked at his leg.

"Please!" squawked Paco. "He's drowning!"

Anders dropped his burrito. "Dude! Drowning? C'mon lil' man! Show me the way!" Paco was already scurrying off. Anders ran after him. "Wait up, chicken little! Wait up, dude!"

Bharat was just ordering the burrito deluxe when he overheard the commotion. He looked down at the silver wrapped delight and up to see the two running down the road. He left the burrito on the counter.

"Wait for me!" he yelled lumbering after them, with Clover at this heels.

[1.44] Under the water, Young Yogi was more content than he had ever been before. He surfed freely and followed his Great-Great-Grandpapa Yoga-ji into the inviting light. For a brief second he recalled the clarity he felt above the clouds in the Magic Meadow. That feeling of the Seed-To-Be was the last memory and thought he had before he surrendered totally to the lure of the light around him now. He surfed easily into the warm glow.

Back at the surface, Paco pointed with his claw, "There! There! He just dropped like a heavy stone. And I don't swim!" He circled in a frenzy.

Anders already had his shirt and shoes off and was heading into the water. "Try to chill, lil' man! I'll get him." Anders hid his worry. He didn't know how long Young Yogi had been under and didn't want to waste another second. "I'm coming, dude!" he said, and took a deep breath and dove into the water.

Bharat came running up, huffing and puffing. "Paco!" he said, wiping the sweat from his brow. "Has he been down long?"

Paco was staring at the ripples created from Ander's dive, his head hanging low. He couldn't speak.

"Don't worry," said Bharat picking the chicken up. "If anyone can save him, you know it's Anders! C'mon, beak up! Don't give up now!" He ruffled Paco's feathers lightly. Bharat felt his throat tense. They both stared at the water and waited.

[1.45] Then Young Yogi's surfboard dissolved away as he watched his Great-Great-Grandpapa Yoga-ji disappear into a blinding, open, and beautiful light. It was so quiet and calm and peaceful. It was perfect. He would go there too.

Anders gulped as he saw the surfboard floating to the surface. He continued on, descending deeper into the water.

[1.46] Young Yogi followed his Great-Great-Grandpapa Yoga-ji into the light, although he was no longer there. Then he felt his body disappear! He could no longer see his shape or that of anything else. He could feel he was merging into something much, much greater than himself. He was without bounds. It felt so natural and normal. It was glorious!

Anders had magnificent lungs and was an expert free diver, but even he began to feel his limitations as he swam into the depths of the water. It was dark and murky and difficult for him to see. He'd have to turn back soon. Where was Young Yogi?

[1.47] Young Yogi was not only immersed in the light, but became part of it. In one way, they seemed to expand outward together while at the same time being at a subtle and unmoving standstill. He felt like an invisible puzzle piece fitting perfectly into an enormous and endless puzzle. Young Yogi had never experienced such clarity before. He had never felt so comfortable and at home. He would happily stay there forever.

Just as Anders felt his last reserves of breath leave him, he spotted Young Yogi tangled in a vast bed of unusual, glowing seaweed. The sight gave him extra air to push on, and he swam faster than ever before. He began to untangle the boy from the long and strange tendrils.

[1.48] In the light world, there were no objects and no words, and yet everyone

and everything in existence was included. Young Yogi had learned in math about infinity, and it was like that. Those were the words and ideas though, and in the light world, there was no need of either. Everything was understood perfectly simply by being a part of everything else.

Anders freed Young Yogi from the strange plant. Seeing his face so serene and happy, Anders knew Yogi was nearly gone for good. Anders began to ascend as quickly as he could.

Back at the water's edge, Bharat said, "Anders has sure been down there a long time. I didn't even think the water was that deep." Paco was fixated on the lake. He knew at some moment its surface would reveal the truth, whatever it may be.

[1.49] Connected to the light, Young Yogi knew the answers to all he had ever questioned. Everything was so simple and clear in the light world. As his understanding emerged, what little remained of the old Young Yogi was slipping away, with no more forms or words necessary.

Anders gasped at the surface. He could feel the dissolved edges of his body return immediately with the inhalation of air. Anyone else would have drowned. Lightheaded, but focused, he lay Young Yogi upon the shore and began clearing his lungs of water. Word spread around town and a crowd of onlookers gathered.

"C'mon lil' dude!" said Anders between pumps on Young Yogi's small chest. "We still have lots of surfin' to do, bro!"

[1.50] There was only love in the great light, and anything he had known prior or since ceased to be. Young Yogi would remain as this vast and luminous universe forever.

Anders tried to breathe air into Young Yogi once again. There was no way he would give up on him. The crowd was silent, and Paco could no longer hold back the well of tears in his eyes as he looked on. Bharat held the chicken tightly.

[1.51] Just as he was about to take that final and invisible step in the pure and perfect light world, the great light flickered, and through it, Young Yogi saw the face of Anders and smiled. He loved Anders!

Just then, Young Yogi coughed up water on the shore. The crowd sighed in relief. Paco jumped up and down from Bharat's arms. Mama and Papa Yogi ran to his side. Young Yogi opened his eyes and saw the great light surrounding his friends and family looking down at him. They were like angels. His heart was full of love and understanding.

"Hi," he said simply with a warm smile. He didn't know why it seemed difficult to speak.

"Dude!" said Anders, "you can't go all the way with the Seed-To-Be just yet lil' dude. We've still got some waves with our names on 'em!" Paco pecked gently on Young Yogi's cheek.

"Hey, Paco," whispered Yogi, happy to see his beloved friend. He was beginning to feel tired all of a sudden.

"Save your words, love," said Mama Yogini cradling his head in her lap. He smiled gently.

"I know . . . I know the place beyond the Mind . . . Monst—" He couldn't speak anymore. He relished in the light and love all around him. It was all he ever needed.

The End

Samādhi Pada

the first book of Patañjali's *Yoga Sūtras*, translated by Luke Jordan

1.1

Now!
This is the instruction of yoga.

1.2

Yoga is . . .
the ending of identification with
the mind's activities.

1.3

Then . . .
the witness
abides in its own true nature.

1.4

Otherwise . . .
there is identification
with the activities.

1.5

The activities come in five forms and cause
distress or non-distress.

1.6

The five forms are . . .
correct perception,
misconception,
imagination,
sleep,
and memory.

1.7

Correct perception comes from . . .
direct experience,
considered reflection,
or from the words of the awakened.

1.8

Misconception [false knowledge]
has no basis in reality.

1.9

Imagination is . . .
an image conjured up through words free
from an underlying source.

1.10
The knowledge of sleep is . . .
based on the absence of any content.

1.11
Memory is . . .
the recollection of past experience.

1.12
These forms and their effects are stilled
through practice
and
non-attachment.

1.13
Practice is . . .
the continued return to resting in steady
lucidity.

1.14
It becomes grounded when
attended to uninterruptedly for a
long period of time.

1.15
Non-attachment is . . .
the letting go of willful seeking after
desired phenomena.

1.16
At its highest, the realization of
consciousness
as separate from
nature
brings desirelessness.

1.17
Awareness then refines through the levels of
discursive thought,
reflective inquiry,
bliss,
and pure "I am"-ness.

1.18
Continued practice leads—beyond this—
to a state in which only
the seeds of past attachments
remain.

1.19
The bodiless
and those merged in nature
still have this seed of re-becoming.

1.20

Others attain the state beyond by means of faith,

strength,

remembrance,

absorption in meditation,

and insight.

1.21

Those who are strongly intense [in practice] are near.

1.22

Hence there are distinctions between mild, moderate, and ardent.

1.23

Or, the state beyond is achieved through surrender to *īśvara*.

1.24

Īśvara is . . .
a separate awareness
untouched by
ignorance, action, its ripening, and residue.

1.25

In that place is
the unsurpassed seed of
all knowing.

1.26

Unlimited by time
īśvara is the *guru* of the
ancient seers.

1.27

Its expression is
ॐ.

1.28

Through repetition
comes understanding of its
meaning.

1.29

Inner awareness is attained,
obstacles disappear.

1.30

These obstacles which distract the mind are:
disease,

dullness,

doubt,

carelessness,

laziness,

indulgence,

confused seeing,

falling back,

instability.

1.31

These distractions are accompanied by:
in the body: suffering and dejection,
in the breath: unsteadiness.

1.32

There is one principle in countering
these distractions:
practice.

1.33

The mind is clarified by cultivating . . .
friendliness toward the happy,
compassion toward those who suffer,
rejoicing toward the virtuous,
indifference toward the wicked.

1.34

Or by . . .
expelling and retaining the breath.

1.35

Or by . . .
binding the mind to
arising sensation.

1.36

Or by . . .
discerning the sorrowless
inner light.

1.37

Or by . . .
freeing the mind of attachments.

1.38

Or by . . .
resting in knowledge derived from sleep.

1.39

Or by . . .
meditating as desired.

1.40

The mastery of one who conquers the mind
extends from
the smallest
to
the greatest.

1.41

With the whirring mind's waning,
it stands clarified
like a precious jewel
reflecting—as one—
experiencer, experiencing, and that which
is experienced.

1.42

At first
knowledge is mixed with
word, concept, and meaning.

1.43

Then,
with memory being purified,
as if emptied of its own form,
meaning alone
—beyond thought—
shines forth.

1.44

So also
knowledge of the subtle begins with reflection
and leads beyond it.

1.45

Such knowledge culminates in
knowing the un-manifest.

1.46

These are *samādhi* with seed.

1.47

With skill, abiding beyond reflection, leads to
the clarity of
the true inner-being.

1.48

In that lies
wisdom of the highest truth.

1.49

With its distinct form
it differs from other forms of knowledge,
"heard" or inferred.

1.50

Impressions born of this knowing
impede the arising of
other impressions.

1.51

In this impression's also ceasing,
from the cessation of all impressions,
there is
samādhi without seed.

Acknowledgments

There are many people who have supported my long journey creating this book. First, thank you to Andrew McAvinchey who encouraged me every murky and marvelous step along the way. I couldn't have done this without him. I'm grateful to Ellen Rouwet, a true guardian angel, whose significant backing was a sign from the universe to keep going. Dena Kingsberg, whose guidance and support far exceeds this project, has been a great blessing in my life.

I have to thank the Committed Practitioners group in Byron Bay, where this idea was born, for their encouragement at the very beginning. I'd also like to thank the Eindhoven yogis for listening to early versions of this story in our *Yoga Sūtras* study group in the Netherlands. I'm also beholden to the yogis in Ireland and the U.S. who were subjected to early drafts of *Young Yogi*. Thank you for listening.

Thank you to Christine McNally, who encouraged this book from the start. Thank you to Maeve Tynan, Jamie Vickers, Nancy Yu, Jackie Fitzpatrick, Ryan Flahive, Marta Lane, Andrada Andrei, Rod Stewart, Yin Yin Wong and the Publication Studio Rotterdam, for perfect advice at the perfect time. My deep appreciation to Gretel Hakanson for serendipitously appearing just when I needed an editor, and fine-tuning an early version of the book. To Lisa Wigutoff Zales, my heartfelt gratitude for her expert assistance, advice and best of all, renewed friendship. A big thanks to Tré Wee and the folks at Publishizer for their efforts and platform. Thank you to Nick Courtright at Atmosphere Press for his focus and enthusiasm in getting this book through the final stages.

I am indebted to all the authors and commentators of various versions of the *Yoga Sūtras*; their comparative wisdom and insights were the backbone of this creation.

I am incredibly grateful and thankful to the talented Kaori Hamura Long whose illustrations and partnership have made Young Yogi a fully tangible reality. Thank you to my mom, Rita Radvila who is always 100% unconditionally supportive. I love you. I have to thank K. Pattabhi Jois and Sharath Jois, and all the yoga teachers who've supported me over the years; without the role of Ashtanga Yoga in my life, this book would not exist at all! Lastly, thank you to my partner and love, Luke Jordan. Without his constant support, positive outlook, good ideas, philosophical and comical support, I would have given up on this long ago.

Thank you to all of our supporters!

SUPER SPONSORS

Gabriella Nicholson/Yoga Tree/Ashtanga Belfast

Luke Jordan

Christina Lagdameo/True Self Yoga

Fieke Klaassen

Jenny Raymundo/Ashtanga Yoga Antwerp

Nick Jones

Rita Radvila

Alison DeMaio

Angela Jamison

Bernadine Rooney

Ester van Winkel

Frédéric de Meyer

Harmony Slater

Joanne Jordan

Magnolia Zuniga

Paul van Malderen

Rachel Nystrom

Shawn Flot

Sonya Barker

Tony Jordan

Victoria Frankel

Cathy Hickey

David Malouin

Eilis O'Broin

Frank Geraerts

SERIOUS SUPPORTERS

Allison Dearling

Anya Milne

Barbara Süss

Bob Seal

Cammy Bean

Chris Whittaker

Christine Mc Nally

Christopher Fenet

Chu & Kelly Calderon

Claudia Pradella

Daria Henning

David Garrigues

Denise Chew

Diana Dixon

Elaine Kirk

Elianne Hoving

Ericka Sparber

Ernesto Riera

Faiza Hassan

Gary Ashley

Georgia Carr

Greg Walsh

Ivica Just

Jackie Fitzpatrick

Jane Lopez

Jenny Lazebnik

Jessica Whelan

Jimmy Helton

Joan Isbell

Joseph Mathers

Karen Kirkness

Katharina Seidler

Katherine Wiedmann

Keith Moore

Leila Garcia

Lisa Zales

Louise Svendsen

Luvenia Maul

Manuel Molina de la Torre

Marion Rovers

Marissa Parareda

Mary Davis

Michelle O'Brien

Ombretta Dettori

Rita Oliveira

Rocio Casas

Romona Mukherjee

Sanne Djaroud-Luesink

Sean Whitley

Shantala Sriramaiah

Siobhan McKenna

Stefanie Jung

Tarik Thami

Tiana Harilela

Tim Feldmann

Tim Hatcher

Tippy Graham

Yara Koberle

FAN CLUB

Ann McDonald	Ann Scott Miller	Edie Berman
Anna De Toni	Anthea Grimason	Elena Kowalski
Anna Costanza	Arancha Sánchez Muñíz	Elisa Paloschi
Astrid Holte Østbye	Arielle Nash	Elizabeth Hauptman
Caroline Labeur	Arne Espejel	Ellen Geljon
Cathy Pearson	Åsa Hermansson	Emese Szecsenyi-Malya
Chris Philson	Audrey Ferrol	Emika Hinden
Cristina Repas	Aurelie Perie	Emma McGinnis
Debby Jägers	Barbara Aparo	Emma Isokivi
Dee Brannigan-Hogarth	Barry Silver	Emma Gorman
Isabel Duesterhoeft	Beata Skrzypacz	Eoghan Masterson
Julia Birkner	Bobby Patterson	Erika Halweil
Kaori Long	Brian Sternkopf	Eva Du Bois
Louise Leonard	Brian Giangardella	Fiona Hynes
Lucy Byatt	Candace Martins	Fiona Walsh
Marese Cregg	Cara Klein	Fleur van Schuylenburch
Maud Gemmeke	Casey Levine	Flora Brajot
Pamela Ramnares	Catherine Moran	Francesca Ameeta Piazzi
Philip Leamy	Chantel Akers	Francis Di Bucchianico-Bakker
Phillip Morgan	Chiara Castellan	Francis Hochstenbach
Pooja Guptar	Chris Kitisakkul	Franziska Guentensperger
Roberta Mozeris	Christine Frontiera	Gail Reisenauer
Sanya Barakova	Christopher Byatt	Gemma Miller
Xamira Möhlmann	Christopher Logel	Gene Hakanson
Yvan Lamelas Polo	Conrad Olivier	Geoffrey Mackenzie
Aaron Green	Constanza Rios	Giuliana Fierro Diaz
Adi Tzur	Corinne Trang	Glenn Bergstrom
Adrian Newkirk	Craig Latimer	Greg Nardi
Aimee Echo	Cristina Estallo	Gwilym Elias
Amy Bear	Crystal Campos	Hamish Hendry
Amy Roulston	Danila Korovin	Hannah Marciniak
Amy Foster	Danny Neumann	Heather Newkirk
Ana Mendes	Dave Miers	Heather Serna
Ana Paula Holtz	David Johnston	Helene Pieren
Andrea Williams	David Eckelkamp	Henriette Macmillan
Andrea Thomson	Dena Wiseman	Hoang Hoa Nguyen
Andreia Martins	Devon Taylor	Holly Menzies
Andrew McAvinchey	Diana Tarré	Inês Pais
Anita Zaupper	Diana Zoto Scavetta	Isabella Nitschke
Ann Svärdfelt	Doreen Wilbers	Jacinta Rankin
Annabelle Rossi	Dorota Pawlak	Jack Simpson
Anne Pinette	Dorothea Zipperle	James Counsellor
Anne Marie Lapointe	Dylan Hendrix	Jean McTigue

Jeanine Goranson	Mandy Beun	Sara Björs
Jeanine Hunter	Manon Simonis	Sarah Brennan
Jennifer Goldstein	Maria Caldwell	Saskia Randt
Jennifer Wade	Maria Burnash	Satish Ramachandran
Jennifer Edwards	Marianna Kedovich	Scott Fischer
Jenny Urice	Mariza Smith	Sean Cleere
Jenny Flatt	Mark McCluskey	Seth Powell
Jeremy Riesenfeld	Marsha McNeight	Sharon McMaster
Jessica Trese	Marta Lane	Shauna Igoe
Jessica Greenfield	Martyna Syguda	Silvie Gausman
Jimmy Van den kieboom	Mary Lyons	Sinead O'Connor
Jimmy Crow	Maureen Thorpe	Sonal Bhalla
Jiri Alexa	Megan Riley	Sonja Duvekot
Joachim Keppel	Meghan Kirk	Sophia Arits
Jon Galpin	Melinda Csapo	Sophie De Vos
Julian di Giovanni	Michael Rawlinson	Stacey Zimet
Juliet Nyatta	Michele Meermans	Stephanie Corigliano
Justin Lippi	Miguel Pons	Stephen Baker
Kaori Long	Miina Suzuki	Steven Harris
Karen Houston	Miluse van de Kant	Susan Therriault
Karina Sun	Molly Lunde	Susan Browne
Katherine Lloyd	Myrna Gonzalez	Susanne Wewerinke
Katrin Eickholt	Natali Kostoska	Suvir Sharma
Keiko Seto	Natalie Evans	Tara Mitra
Kerstin Sääw	Nicholas Evans	Taraneh Entezami
Kerstin Bilgmann	Nicole Elliott	Theresa Gulliver
Khristine Jones	Nikki Cousins	Thomas O'Reilly
Kim Evans	Olga Lazareva	Tom Powell
Kris Brothers	Paola Orlando	Tré Wee
Kristin Devine	Patricia Moore	Wei Li
Lara Lauchheimer	Patrick Nolan	Yuka Higashino
Laura Pero	Paula McCartney	Yvonne Link
Laurah Klepinger	Peter Yribia	Zephyr Mercer
Laurissa Vibhuti	Peter Taminiau	Zoe Slatoff
Leonard Truong	Pia Wintschnig	
Leonardo Carneiro	Priscila Barradas	
Leonie Kriellaars	Priya Jhawar	
Lesley Dow	Prue Keenan	
Lisa Goodrich	Raymond Lammerts van Bueren	
Lisa Janssen	Robert Muratore	
Lissa Borchers	Robin Wolfson	
Lorena Gaibor	Ron van der Vlist	
Lorraine Taylor	Rosangela Castellari	
Lucia Letkova	Rosie McMahon	
Lucie Wurst	Ryan Doran	
Lusiena Dudnik	Samantha Harkin	
Maike Heesakkers	Sanja Dol-Lazarevic	

About the Author

Born and raised in Colorado, Sonja Radvila has always had a deep curiosity about the world, creativity, and inner transformation. After studying film production and anthropology at the University of Colorado in Boulder, and the American University in Cairo, Egypt, she went on to become a video editor for television for 8 ½ years, working at Starz! and The Discovery Channel. It was her first visit to Chennai, India in 1999 that deeply affected the course of her life. While intensively studying Bharata Natyam, a classical Indian dance form, she was introduced to her first experiences of yoga with daily classes in asana, chanting, and pranayama, at the local Sivananda Ashram. A year later she resonated with her first Ashtanga yoga class, which joined movement and breath in a new and profound way, one that would carry her to the present day. Since 2004, she has maintained a daily practice in that tradition, making nearly annual visits to study at the heart of the Ashtanga practice at the KPJAYI, in Mysore, India. She has been sharing the system of Ashtanga yoga since 2008, teaching internationally, and has been an authorized teacher since 2010.

In addition to her love of yoga and dance, Sonja enjoys writing, art, photography, reading, cooking, health and consciousness exploration, nature, and animals. She is also the founder and creator of Rasa Malas which specializes in intuitively designed jewelry and unique vintage jewelry from India. She currently resides in Portugal.

www.youngyogiworld.com
www.sonjaradvila.com

About the Illustrator

Kaori Hamura Long is an artist and illustrator who has many TV and film credits, including MTV's *Beavis and Butt-head*, *MTV Downtown*, *Daria*, and Nickelodeon's *Gary the Rat*. She also created MTV's Video Music Award packaging animation and MTV2 Station I.D. She has done numerous magazine illustrations for *New York Press*, *Time Out*, *Interview Magazine*, *Mademoiselle*, *RayGun*, *CosmoGIRL!* and others. She has also done T-shirt designs for Anna Sui, Patricia Field, and Liquid Sky Records.

She was born in Fukuoka, Japan, and graduated from Parsons School of Design. Her pilot animation, *Bootie Boogie*, was aired on Oxygen. Bootie Boogie has won a Silver Award for The Society of Illustrators' Annual Awards 2003 in Los Angeles. She has established a creative company, Moss Moon Studio, with Bill Long. Currently, she is developing children's books and book apps. Aside from making art, she loves hiking, gardening and spending time with her family.

About Atmosphere Press

Atmosphere Press is an independent, full-service publisher for books in genres ranging from nonfiction to fiction to poetry, with a special emphasis on being an author-friendly approach to the challenges of getting a book into the world. Learn more about what we do at atmospherepress.com.

We encourage you to check out some of Atmosphere's latest releases, which are available at Amazon.com and via order from your local bookstore:

the oneness of Reality, poetry by Brock Mehler
Difficulty Swallowing, essays by Kym Cunningham
Come Kill Me!, short stories by Mackinley Greenlaw
The Unexpected Aneurysm of the Potato Blossom Queen, short stories by Garrett Socol
Gathered, a novel by Kurt Hansen
Interviews from the Last Days, sci-fi poetry by Christina Loraine
Unorthodoxy, a novel by Joshua A.H. Harris
The Clockwork Witch, a young adult novel by McKenzie P. Odom
Frank, a novel by Gina DeNicola
My WILD First Day of School, a picture book by Dennis Mathew
Drop Dead Red, poetry by Elizabeth Carmer
Aging Without Grace, poetry by Sandra Fox Murphy
A User Guide to the Unconscious Mind, nonfiction by Tatiana Lukyanova
The Sky Belongs to the Dreamers, a picture book by J.P. Hostetler
I Will Love You Forever and Always, a picture book by Sarah Thomas Mariano
Shooting Stars: A Girls Can Do Anything Book, children's fiction by Carmen Petro
The George Stories, a novel by Christopher Gould
No Home Like a Raft, poetry by Martin Jon Porter
Mere Being, poetry by Barry D. Amis
The Traveler, a young adult novel by Jennifer Deaver
Breathing New Life: Finding Happiness after Tragedy, nonfiction by Bunny Leach

Oscar the Loveable Seagull, a picture book by Mark Johnson

Mandated Happiness, a novel by Clayton Tucker

The Third Door, a novel by Jim Williams

The Yoga of Strength, a novel by Andrew Marc Rowe

They are Almost Invisible, poetry by Elizabeth Carmer

Let the Little Birds Sing, a novel by Sandra Fox Murphy

Carpenters and Catapults: A Girls Can Do Anything Book, children's fiction by Carmen Petro

Spots Before Stripes, a novel by Jonathan Kumar

Auroras over Acadia, poetry by Paul Liebow

Channel: How to be a Clear Channel for Inspiration by Listening, Enjoying, and Trusting Your Intuition, nonfiction by Jessica Ang

Gone Fishing: A Girls Can Do Anything Book, children's fiction by Carmen Petro

Owlfred the Owl, a picture book by Caleb Foster

Love Your Vibe: Using the Power of Sound to Take Command of Your Life, nonfiction by Matt Omo

Transcendence, poetry and images by Vincent Bahar Towliat

Leaving the Ladder: An Ex-Corporate Girl's Guide from the Rat Race to Fulfilment, nonfiction by Lynda Bayada

Adrift, poems by Kristy Peloquin

Time Do Not Stop, poems by William Guest

Dear Old Dogs, a novella by Gwen Head

Bello the Cello, a picture book by Dennis Mathew

How Not to Sell: A Sales Survival Guide, nonfiction by Rashad Daoudi

Ghost Sentence, poems by Mary Flanagan

That Scarlett Bacon, a picture book by Mark Johnson

Makani and the Tiki Mikis, a picture book by Kosta Gregory

What Outlives Us, poems by Larry Levy

Winter Park, a novel by Graham Guest

That Beautiful Season, a novel by Sandra Fox Murphy

What I Cannot Abandon, poems by William Guest

All the Dead Are Holy, poems by Larry Levy

Surviving Mother, a novella by Gwen Head

Who Are We: Man and Cosmology, poetry by William Guest